# Moments of Edification

## Volume 1

### VERONICA DIXON

Book Cover Design: Prize Publishing House

Printed by: Prize Publishing House, LLC in the United States of America.

First printing edition 2023.

Prize Publishing House
P.O. Box 9856, Chesapeake, VA 23321
www.PrizePublishingHouse.com

Library of Congress Control Number: 2023907477

ISBN (Paperback): 979-8-9875046-6-6
ISBN (E-Book): 979-8-9875046-7-3

# CONTENTS

*Day 1*

# CLEAR THE ROOM

## (Fill My Space With You)

L ife happens to us all. The hustle and bustle of each day clouds our thoughts and tries to inject worry and fear. The long "To Do" List often causes our world to spin and makes us forget to invite God into our day. The expectations of others demand us to perform, and the daily responsibilities overload us with anxiety.

During these times, we must stop and realize that we can not do anything without Him. We can't perform, meet expectations, or be our best selves. At this point, we need to pause and ask Him to fill our space with Him. When His presence shows up, we are able to do what we thought we were incapable of doing; *His presence is accompanied by everything we need.* His presence brings comfort, joy, and direction. Whatever we need, we now have access to it.

*Whenever your space is filled with busyness, worry, or the feeling of being overwhelmed, pause and ask Him to CLEAR the room and fill your space with His presence.*

Invite Him in. He is waiting.

# Scriptures

*"You will show me the way of life, granting me the joy of your presence and the pleasures of living with you forever."*
– Psalm 16:11

*"For the LORD your God is living among you. He is a mighty savior. He will take delight in you with gladness. With his love, he will calm all your fears. He will rejoice over you with joyful songs."*
– Zephaniah 3:17

# Prayer

God, You are the one I come to when my mind is cloudy, and my strength is depleted. You are the one I run to when I don't know where to place my foot next. Invade my space with Your peace, direction, and joy. When Your presence shows up, it demands everything to change. Your presence calms every one of my fears and reassures me of Your plan for my life. Thank You for removing everything out of my space that shouldn't be there and filling my space with You.

# *Day 2*
# FIRST INSTINCT

I nstinct is a way of behaving, thinking, or feeling that is not learned. Instinct is a natural desire or tendency that makes you want to respond in a particular way. What is your first instinct when bad things happen or when everything is chaotic and falling apart?

Is your first instinct to worry, speak things contrary to His word, and give in to the pressure, or is your first instinct to invite God in on it, not allow it to overtake you, and trust God despite all opposition? What is your first instinct?

Trust comes naturally to those who have a history with God. *To those who have a history with God, trust is their first instinct.* It is their first instinct because they look back at every adversity He gave them victory over. They reminisce on all the times He kept His promise; therefore, they respond with the most reliable thing they know, trusting Him. When you have tested and tried something, you can properly validate it.

When you face adversity, ask God to let your first instinct be to immediately trust Him and be fully persuaded that He is capable of performing every word He has spoken.

# Scriptures

*"Trust in the LORD and do good. Then you will live safely in the land and prosper."*
– Psalm 37:3

*"Those who know your name trust in you, for you, O LORD, do not abandon those who search for you."*
- Psalm 9:10

# Affirmation

I trust You to fix what I can't. You are capable and reliable. I trust You with my life. It is Your will to do me good. You will not fail me.

*Day 3*

# CLOSER THAN CLOSE

When you are in the thick of it, know that He is near. This is the time He is closer than close. He may feel distant and so far away, but He is there in the midst of everything with you. When you open your eyes in the morning and don't want to get out of bed, He is near. When your thoughts are cloudy from the turmoil, He is near. When you feel the unction to relieve some of the pressure but don't have the strength to, *He is still right there in the middle of everything with you.*

God is in the midst, ready to assist you, bring you relief, and order your every step. This is when your faith must activate, and you must cling to EVERY word He has said. Lean into His word, cling to it, and take Him at His word. He is a reliable source that is ready to come to your aid. He is near and is as close as the mention of His name.

# Scriptures

"But as for me, how good it is to be near God! I have made the Sovereign LORD my shelter, and I will tell everyone about the wonderful things you do."
– Psalm 73:28

"May the LORD our God be with us as he was with our ancestors; may he never leave us or abandon us."
– 1 Kings 8:57

"The LORD is close to all who call on him, yes, to all who call on him in truth."
– Psalm 145:18

# Prayer

Father, thank You for walking through every trial and disappointment with me. I thank You that I am never alone. You are there to bring me peace, hope, and strength. Today I rejoice that You are in this with me and that You are closer than close. When I want to give up, I ask that You continue to remind me of Your presence.

# Day 4
# DON'T TOUCH IT

## (Give It To Me)

**W**e are all guilty of saying, *God, don't let one more thing happen because if it does, I am going to scream.* Then we look up, and that one more thing happens. Surprisingly, we don't scream because we finally realize this is beyond our control. *I mean, what can we do? How can we fix it? How can we make this right?* We can't! Because it's a job for the Great Jehovah.

**Some things we can't touch. Only He can. He is the only one who can touch it and make it right.** Therefore, we have to leave it alone and commit it to Him. Oftentimes, when we try to deal with things within our own strength, we make it worse. It then brings on frustration. Frustration comes because it is not for us to deal with. He is looking at us struggling with it, and saying, "Lay it at my feet. This is too big for you. This is too heavy for you to carry."

The minute we realize that our God specializes in the impossible is the minute we will stop touching situations we shouldn't and allow God to do all the heavy lifting. God is looking at us and saying, "I am the Lord, the God of all flesh; is there anything too difficult for Me?" We will respond with "No," but our actions will speak louder, saying something different. If we really believed God and took Him at His word, we would give Him the situation and let Him do what He does best - the impossible.

# Scriptures

"Don't worry about anything; instead, pray about everything. Tell God what you need, and thank him for all he has done. Then you will experience God's peace, which exceeds anything we can understand. His peace will guard your hearts and minds as you live in Christ Jesus."
– Philippians 4:6-7

"O Sovereign LORD! You made the heavens and earth by your strong hand and powerful arm. Nothing is too hard for you!"
– Jeremiah 32:17

# Prayer

Heavenly Father, I come to You, committing every one of my problems to You. They are not designed for me to carry. You specialize in the impossible. You are the God of miracles, signs, and wonders. I thank You that nothing is too difficult for You and that You have already moved on my behalf.

*Day 5*

# DANGER ZONE

There are some things that people can do, and it appears they get away with it. They feel they are justified and have no Godly conviction about their actions. Sometimes their actions are supported by an audience placing their stamp of approval to solidify the behavior.

There have been times when those of us who love God come along and attempt to mimic the exact behavior, and it doesn't work that way for us. We then begin to wonder why we can't do what we want. Why can't we do things without feeling grieved or convicted? The second we do things, the Holy Spirit immediately begins to speak, and we become Godly sorry.

At this point, we realize we can't do what we want, say what we want, or even go where we want because our life is not our own. The minute we step outside His will, we feel His displeasure and hear His voice speaking loudly, directing us back.

While others celebrate that they can do what they want, we don't feel the liberty to do so. Whenever we cross the line, we feel like we have stepped into the danger zone. Well, here's the good news about that. Rejoice that you don't feel free to do what you want because that signifies you have a Godly conviction that constrains you and alerts you when you have crossed the line. ***Whenever you lose your Godly conviction, you have stepped into the danger zone and are no longer safe.***

# Scriptures

*"There is a path before each person that
seems right, but it ends in death."*
– Proverbs 14:12

*"Stay on the path that the Lord your God has commanded
you to follow. Then you will live long and prosperous lives
in the land you are about to enter and occupy."*
– Deuteronomy 5:33

*"Guide my steps by your word,
so I will not be overcome by evil."*
– Psalm 119:133

# Prayer

Lord, I ask that You show me Your way. Let me clearly hear
Your voice and follow. Let me gladly delight in doing the
things that bring glory to Your name. When I am tempted to
do things my way, quickly bring on a Godly conviction and
make my spirit subject to You. I want to honor You in all I
say and do. I want to live my life for You. You are my life.

# Day 6

# I AM THE ANSWER

Has anyone ever told you *God sent you my way, you showed up at the right time, or you know exactly what to do or say?* If so, what they are saying is, *you are the answer to my prayers. I prayed about this, and God sent you.* **What an honor to be a gift that God gives to others!**

One of our personal prayers should be, *Lord, let me be the answer to someone's prayers. When someone comes in contact with me, let me have what they need. If they feel despair, let them instantly feel there is hope. If they feel alone, let them suddenly feel the comfort of the Comforter. If they feel lost, let them find their footing and know where to place each step. If a need is pressing, let that need be supplied.*

**When we desire to be the answer to someone's prayer, we are telling God that we have chosen to live a selfless life.** Living a selfless life is a life that considers others and prioritizes the needs of others and not just our own. A selfless life recognizes and understands that they are often the answer to other people's prayers. People who live selflessly count it an honor to serve God's people. They wake up every day ready to pour into others. They realize that God has favored them to be the answer.

## Scripture

*"God has given each of you a gift from his great variety of spiritual gifts. Use them well to serve one another. Do you have the gift of speaking? Then speak as though God himself were speaking through you. Do you have the gift of helping others? Do it with all the strength and energy that God supplies. Then everything you do will bring glory to God through Jesus Christ. All glory and power to him forever and ever! Amen."*
– 1 Peter 4:10-11

## Prayer

God, if they are looking for You, let them find You in me. Let my life be the road map leading to You. Let Your everlasting love beaming through me be what draws, keeps, and sustains them. Keep my cup full and overflowing so that the abundance of Your peace and joy spill over to all I come in contact with.

I thank You for choosing me to be the answer to someone's prayers and for finding me worthy enough to serve Your people.

# Day 7

# IN PURSUIT OF YOU

Everyone is pursuing something, and everyone has their reason for pursuing that one thing. If we asked each person what they are in pursuit of and why, each person's answer and motive would be different. Some are in pursuit of happiness, while others have placed money, fame, or a great name at the top of their list.

Many have pursued success, and once they achieve it, they still feel empty, alone, and unhappy because they have failed to understand that God is the only one who can make them feel whole, secure, and have joy that overflows. We find all those things in Him and in doing what He has assigned us to do.

When we chase the wrong things, God will not receive the glory out of our lives, and we are on a road engulfed with unhappiness. If that is the case, why even pursue it?

We need to ask God to shift our desires and help us realize that everything we need is in Him. If we pursue Him - meaning, His will, His way, and His plan. We will have everything we need. When we pursue Him, we have made Him our desire, wanting Him more than anything. *Put Him first and pursue the things that bring Him honor. As you honor Him, He will honor you.*

# Scriptures

*"Seek the Kingdom of God above all else, and live righteously, and he will give you everything you need."*
– Matthew 6:33

*"O God, you are my God; I earnestly search for you. My soul thirsts for you; my whole body longs for you in this parched and weary land where there is no water."*
– Psalm 63:1

# Prayer

Father, I ask that You forgive me for chasing the wrong things and for wanting and placing things before You. I realize that all I need is You. If I have You, I have everything. You are my desire. As I seek you, all things will be added unto me.

# Affirmation

I am in pursuit of You. I seek You. I have made You a priority. I have placed You first. You are the God of my choice. Nothing will separate me from Your love.

# Day 8
# ONLY FOR A MOMENT

There is a saying that trouble doesn't last always. This sounds cliche, but if you, *Selah* - pause and calmly think, this is true. When you are in the middle of your trouble, it may feel like an eternity with no ending date. The devil desires you to think there is no ending date so that the pressures of your trouble can cause you to faint.

During these times, you must let what God said to resonate in your heart. You must let His word fill your heart so you can rest in Him. When we rest in God, it is a place of trust. It's a place wherein we know we are safe because we have chosen to take Him at His word.

In life, we go through seasons, but we must know seasons change. Some seasons are cold, bitter, and full of rain, but if we endure hardness as good soldiers and don't faint, we will see the changing of that season. We will see the clouds dissipate and the sun breaking through, symbolizing the breaking of day and a new season.

Trouble is designed to make you fear, lose hope, and collapse. Don't give in to any of those tactics. Know that God is near and with You. Whenever we experience trouble, He is in the midst.

**Don't look at the problem. When the devil gives you a problem, you are supposed to give that problem to God.** Know that every problem has an expiration date. So wait for it! You have an expected end.

# Scriptures

*"For there is a time and a way for everything,*
*even when a person is in trouble."*
– Ecclesiastes 8:6

*"Wait patiently for the LORD. Be brave and*
*courageous. Yes, wait patiently for the LORD."*
– Psalm 27:14

*"As for me, I look to the LORD for help. I wait confidently*
*for God to save me, and my God will certainly hear me."*
– Micah 7:7

*"We put our hope in the LORD. He is our help and our shield. In*
*him our hearts rejoice, for we trust in his holy name. Let your*
*unfailing love surround us, LORD, for our hope is in you alone."*
– Psalm 33:20-21

# Prayer

When troubles arise, help me to know that they are
only for a moment. Remind me that You are with me by
allowing me to feel Your presence. I thank You that Your
presence will bring me peace and strength. During these
times, remind me of Your word, which is Your promise.
Let me stand firm in You, waiting for this cup to pass.

# *Day 9*

# LOVING THE UNLOVABLE

When you really love God, He shows you how to love the unlovable. Through Him, we learn to love others despite their situation or how they treat us. God knew that we would encounter people who are not easy to love. That's why he commanded us to love our neighbors as ourselves.

When we look at people, the devil wants us to see all their flaws and why they are not easy to love. It may be their attitude, way of thinking, personality, or how they treat us. It may even be that they deeply offended us. Whatever it may be, all their flaws are magnified, and they are not easy to love.

What do you do when you have been commanded to love the unlovable? First, you need to remember how much you've been loved and extended grace. Then extend that same love and grace to them that was freely extended to you by God and others. Remember, we are all imperfect people serving a perfect God. Our expectation should never be that everyone should have it all together. Those are unrealistic expectations. We are all flawed.

Finally, you need to pray for your own heart, asking God for a heart like His. *A heart like His equals a love like His.* His heart forgives quickly, willingly extends grace, and is patient. These are some of the characteristics of God's heart.

*If you have difficulty loving others, fall in love with Him, and He will show you how to love them.* After all, it is a love thing. We have been commanded to do so.

# Scriptures

"This is my commandment: Love each other
in the same way I have loved you."
– John 15:12

"Love is patient and kind. Love is not jealous or boastful or proud or
rude. It does not demand its own way. It is not irritable, and it keeps
no record of being wronged. It does not rejoice about injustice but
rejoices whenever the truth wins out. Love never gives up, never loses
faith, is always hopeful, and endures through every circumstance."
– Corinthians 13:4-7

"Dear friends, let us continue to love one another, for love comes
from God. Anyone who loves is a child of God and knows God. But
anyone who does not love does not know God, for God is love."
– 1 John 4:7-8

# Affirmation

I will my spirit to love like You. I will my spirit to forgive
like You. I will extend grace and compassion to those
who offend me. My love is a mirror of Your love.

# *Day 10*

# THE STAIN OF SHAME

All of us have experienced distress and humiliation from doing something wrong. The feeling of guilt makes us want to hide and never come out. We then begin to beat ourselves up and allow the enemy to tell us how we are no longer worthy of being used by God or valuable enough to have any good thing come to us. When the truth is *God's grace is greater than our sins. He has enough grace to cover us.*

*The stain of shame will try to attach itself to us. If we allow it, it will diminish our self-worth and deem us invaluable.* God wants us to release the shame and know that we are loved beyond measure and that His blood has washed away every past mistake. He wants us to know that we are new creatures in Him and that all things are made new.

When the enemy tries to make you feel guilt and shame, know that God has erased all of your shame. Replace those shame-filled thoughts with God's word, which is truth.

# Scriptures

*"Fear not; you will no longer live in shame. Don't be afraid;
there is no more disgrace for you. You will no longer remember
the shame of your youth and the sorrows of widowhood."*
– Isaiah 54:4

*"As the Scriptures tell us, 'Anyone who trusts
in him will never be disgraced.'"*
– Romans 10:11

# Affirmation

Shame will not hold me hostage. God's grace is
enough to cover me. Shame will no longer stop
me from my purpose. God has need of me.

# *Day 11*

# LOVE ON DISPLAY

God's love is infallible. Daily, His love is displayed. Each day that He breathes life into us, His love is demonstrated. The way He provides for us when there is a need and how He touches our hearts when they are broken solidifies His love and removes all questions. His love makes us feel secure and protected.

*God's love is so tangible we can't deny it.* The truth is, He wants us to feel His love. He wants us to feel surrounded and overwhelmed by it. So overwhelmed that we want to return the love. *Real love reciprocates. Real love responds with gratitude, thankfulness, and obedience to His word.*

How can we express our love to Him? How can we convey our true thoughts and feelings toward Him? What can we say to let Him know how we feel?

We can convey what comes to our hearts and mind, but it's not so much in what we say; it's in everything we do. The way we show God we love Him is through our obedience. Obeying what His word says proves our love for Him. It shows God we are willing to abandon our agenda, trust what He said and do things His way. *Obedience is our highest level of worship.*

If we want to display our authentic love for God, obedience is key. *Obedience is God's love language.*

# Scriptures

*"Those who accept my commandments and obey them are the ones who love me. And because they love me, my Father will love them. And I will love them and reveal myself to each of them." Judas (not Judas Iscariot, but the other disciple with that name) said to him, "Lord, why are you going to reveal yourself only to us and not to the world at large?" Jesus replied, "All who love me will do what I say. My Father will love them, and we will come and make our home with each of them. Anyone who doesn't love me will not obey me. And remember, my words are not my own. What I am telling you is from the Father who sent me."*
– John 14:21-24

*"Loving God means keeping his commandments, and his commandments are not burdensome."*
– 1 John 5:3

# Prayer

Dear God, today I come asking that You lead me. Let me follow what Your word says. Let Your word be a lamp unto my feet and a light unto my path. I thank You that my spirit has been conditioned to hear and obey Your word. I thank You that the more I obey You, the closer I get to You. My obedience is drawing me closer to You. I thank You that even when I want to walk in my own way, You quickly convict me, and I am reminded of what Your word says.

# Day 12
## TAG, YOU'RE IT!

Tag! You're it! It was nothing like hearing that when you were running and playing with your friends on the playground. That symbolized that it was your turn. It was now your turn to chase after the next person. It may sound like it was no fun because you were chasing after another person, but it was all fun, and you loved every bit of it. Especially when you could tag the next person and let them know it is now their turn.

Well, are you ready for this? God has tagged some of us and told us it is now our turn. Yes! It is our turn! It is our turn to come from the back to the front, to operate in our gifts, and do great exploits in His name. He has taken us from the bottom and placed us on top. It is now time for Him to receive the glory for the gifts He has placed in our earthen vessels.

When God tags you, it will sometimes put you in an uncomfortable place. But push past every feeling of discomfort and go forth because it's your turn. Don't miss the moment!

## Scriptures

*"You didn't choose me. I chose you. I appointed you to go and produce lasting fruit, so that the Father will give you whatever you ask for, using my name."*
– John 15:16

*"For you are a holy people, who belong to the LORD your God. Of all the people on earth, the LORD your God has chosen you to be his own special treasure."*
– Deuteronomy 7:6

## Affirmation

I have been chosen. It is now my turn. I yield to Your will. Here is my life. Use it. I will not miss this moment.

*Day 13*

# TOO ANOINTED TO QUIT

When life gets crazy and all out of sorts, it can be very tempting to want to quit. The pressure to perform and hang in there can get so thick that quitting suddenly becomes an option.

When we become weary in well-doing, satan uses that to make us feel unproductive and defeated. He magnifies every opposition we face so that the stress of it all seems unbearable. So unbearable that we forget our assignment. We even forget the mere fact that He anointed us for this.

During times like these, it is time to lean in with prayer and draw closer to God, our rock. He is our stabilizer. He is the one who holds our world together and makes us steadfast. As we draw closer to Him, He will draw closer to us. He will then impart the portion of strength needed to withstand every trial. He will remind us how we have been set apart and chosen; therefore, quitting is not an option because we are too anointed to quit.

# Scriptures

*"I press on to reach the end of the race and receive the heavenly prize for which God, through Christ Jesus, is calling us."*
– Philippians 3:14

*"But as for you, be strong and courageous, for your work will be rewarded."*
– 2 Chronicles 15:7

*"So let's not get tired of doing what is good. At just the right time we will reap a harvest of blessing if we don't give up."*
– Galatians 6:9

# Prayer

Heavenly Father, thank You for giving me the spirit of a finisher. I thank You for imparting strength and grit in me so that I won't abandon my assignment. When things get hard and I become weary, I thank You that I can run to Your arms for rest. You are my refuge and safe place. With You, I can face it all.

*Day 14*

# YOU HAVE MY FULL SUPPORT

For every assignment that God has given us, He is counting on us to fulfill it and not drop the ball. He is looking at us, saying, "I have placed everything you need inside of you to complete this. Don't doubt yourself or your gift. I have groomed you for this moment. I am here to assist you in carrying this out." What God is saying is, *You have my full support.*

When we have God's full support, we no longer should search for the support or validation of others. He is all we need. His seal of approval is an automatic green light to proceed. So, why do we feel like that isn't enough?

Often, when God has given us an assignment, our success is based upon what others think, how they feel or what they would do. When the truth is, the need for others' approval should hold no value because God has already said, *you have My full support.*

When we have His support, nothing else matters. His support should remove all fear, second-guessing, and the need for validation. God's stamp of approval is the final authority.

# Scriptures

*"Don't be afraid, for I am with you. Don't be discouraged,*
*for I am your God. I will strengthen you and help you. I*
*will hold you up with my victorious right hand."*
– Isaiah 41:10

*"The LORD helps them, rescuing them from the wicked.*
*He saves them, and they find shelter in him."*
– Psalm 37:40

*"We put our hope in the LORD. He is our help and our shield."*
– Psalm 33:20

# Affirmation

You are my shield. I trust You to uphold and support me. My
hope is in You. No good thing will You withhold from me.

# Day 15

# THE JOURNEY

Before He formed the world, we were on His mind. He knows our beginning to the end. That's why He is called "Alpha and Omega." We can be at the start of something, and He already knows the end. We often get afraid because we can't see the journey that leads to the end, but that's what faith is. Faith is trusting what we can't see.

We want to know every detail, every possible stumbling block, and anything that could be a hindrance. We want all the details so we can plan, be prepared, and brace ourselves. God won't always give all the details because He is trying to take us to a place of "Trusting Him Only." If He gave us all the details, this would defeat the purpose of the journey.

Walking with God can sometimes be like traveling to a destination with no road map. You don't know whether you are going north or south. You don't know how far to travel down the road, and you definitely don't know the final destination. You don't have all the details; therefore, you must trust His leading and follow the leader. A journey like this can be scary, but He takes us on journeys like this so that we are confident that He is a good leader. It is a faith-building journey. Faith-building journeys are necessary. Faith is a muscle that only gets stronger if we exercise it.

So next time God takes you on a journey, and He doesn't tell you the beginning to end, trust His leading and the process. We can't see our way, but we can trust it - because He is trustworthy.

# Scriptures

*"As the Scriptures tell us, 'Anyone who trusts in him will never be disgraced.'"*
– Romans 10:11

*"'For I know the plans I have for you,' says the LORD. 'They are plans for good and not for disaster, to give you a future and a hope.'"*
– Jeremiah 29:11

# Prayer

Heavenly Father, help me to trust Your leading. I ask that You help me follow You, even when I can't see my way. As you lead, help me to cling to Your word. Your word will forever stand. Show me where to place each step. You are the leader. I am the follower. I trust Your leading and know it will bring me to a safe place filled with Your goodness.

# *Day 16*

# GIVE WHAT YOU NEED

We have all heard *I can't help them because I need help* or *I can't support them because I need support.* We have even heard, *how can I encourage them when I need encouragement?* This is the time to practice giving what you need.

Often God will put us in situations where we are required to give what we need. He will challenge us to be someone's strength when we need strength. He will challenge us to intercede for others when we need intercession done on our behalf. He will challenge us to show someone the way when we can't see the way He has set before us. This type of challenge stretches us because it requires us to become selfless. It makes one think, *how can I help someone else when I feel I don't have a sufficient supply of everything I need?* Isn't that like God? While we are standing with questions. He already has all of the answers.

God's ways are not our ways, neither His thoughts our thoughts. He sees our needs and will challenge us to pour into others because He knows that as we pour into others, He will pour back into us. Pouring into others puts a demand on God to pour back into us. God promised that when we pour into others, He will restore and strengthen us. This is proof that there is power in serving others.

When we edify, empower, support, and inspire others, we are His hands, feet, and mouthpiece. So be that listening ear, pray the prayer of faith over those who are weak, provide support to those who feel alone, and speak words that bring life to those who have lost their way. You may need everything you are giving, but stretch yourself and give it anyway. As you give it, He will give it back to you. This is the law of reciprocity.

# Scriptures

"Feed the hungry, and help those in trouble. Then your light will shine out from the darkness, and the darkness around you will be as bright as noon. The LORD will guide you continually, giving you water when you are dry and restoring your strength. You will be like a well-watered garden, like an ever-flowing spring."
– Isaiah 58:10-11

"When God's people are in need, be ready to help them. Always be eager to practice hospitality."
– Romans 12:13

"Don't be selfish; don't try to impress others. Be humble, thinking of others as better than yourselves. Don't look out only for your own interests, but take an interest in others, too. You must have the same attitude that Christ Jesus had."
– Philippians 2:3-5

# Prayer

Heavenly Father, I thank You that even at my lowest point, when I see others hurt, wounded, or in need of support, I will become selfless and give them what I need. I thank You for Your word that says as I pour into others, You will restore and strengthen me. Let my heart always be sensitive to Your people and discerning of their needs. I thank You that I will always be a vessel that You flow through.

# Day 17

# FULLY EQUIPPED

God gives His toughest battles to His strongest soldiers. When things get heated, overwhelming, and too heavy to bear, you literally feel like fainting from the weight of it all. The weight of it causes your anxiety to be on overload, making way for doubt and questions to creep in. Questions like, why me? When will this be over? What purpose will this serve? All of these questions make you feel as if God has forsaken you. When the truth is, He is so close.

Certain battles make you hold your emotions in for fear others will doubt your faith and question whether you really believe in the God you serve. They fail to understand that some situations knock the wind out of you. They are not aware that you are holding on with everything inside of you. Silently praying that someone will feel your devastation, hear your silent scream and come to your rescue, but no one does, so you go through in silence while the feeling of loneliness overshadows you.

In moments like these, you must know that although you feel weak, you are strong. We now can bear witness when Paul said, 'Therefore I will boast all the more gladly about my weaknesses, so that Christ's power may rest on me." His power is now resting upon you, giving you everything you need.

God allows certain things to be so because He has given us the strength to endure them; therefore, we have everything we need and are fully equipped. This is so like God! *When you are in a battle, He has already equipped you with everything you need to obtain the victory. No soldier ever goes to a battle unequipped.* You are more prepared than you think. You are stronger than you think. It is now time to dig deep, gird yourself up on your most holy faith and put on your armor because you are equipped for it all.

# Scriptures

"By his divine power, God has given us everything we
need for living a godly life. We have received all of this
by coming to know him, the one who called us to himself
by means of his marvelous glory and excellence."
– 2 Peter 1:3

"May he equip you with all you need for doing his will. May he
produce in you, through the power of Jesus Christ, every good thing
that is pleasing to him. All glory to him forever and ever! Amen."
– Hebrews 13:21

"Put on all of God's armor so that you will be able to stand firm
against all strategies of the devil. For we are not fighting against flesh-
and-blood enemies, but against evil rulers and authorities of the unseen
world, against mighty powers in this dark world, and against evil
spirits in the heavenly places. Therefore, put on every piece of God's
armor so you will be able to resist the enemy in the time of evil. Then
after the battle you will still be standing firm. Stand your ground,
putting on the belt of truth and the body armor of God's righteousness.
For shoes, put on the peace that comes from the Good News so that
you will be fully prepared. In addition to all of these, hold up the
shield of faith to stop the fiery arrows of the devil. Put on salvation
as your helmet, and take the sword of the Spirit, which is the word
of God. Pray in the Spirit at all times and on every occasion. Stay
alert and be persistent in your prayers for all believers everywhere."
– Ephesians 6:11-18

## Affirmation

God has not forsaken me. Fear has no power over me. I
have taken the power of fear away by standing on His
word. He is with me. I am fully equipped for everything
I may experience. Victory is assigned to me.

# Day 18

# MY LIFE IS FOR HIS PERSONAL USE

The world is chanting. It's your life, so live it! The slogan, "You only live once," is on shirts, hats, and plastered everywhere. The pressure to find and do what makes you happy is being enforced and used as a motto for people to live by. *Doing what brings you joy is trending. But what if what brings you joy brings God sorrow?*

While some things are good, that doesn't mean we have a green light to do them. Many things may look, feel and sound good but is that part of God's plan for your life? *Everyone has their agenda, but a true follower of Christ will put their agenda away and say, my life is for His personal use. Meaning, here's my life, Lord, I yield to Your will. What will You have me do? My life is set aside for Your personal use. While these other things are enticing, Your plan for my life trumps all other plans.*

When we tell God our lives are set aside for His personal use, we are saying we have dedicated our lives to Him. We have made ourselves available to be used by Him, and we have forsaken our will in exchange for His. This is the heart posture of those who have totally surrendered to Him.

# Scriptures

"You say, 'I am allowed to do anything' —but not everything is good for you. You say, 'I am allowed to do anything'—but not everything is beneficial."
- 1 Corinthians 10:23

"If we live, it's to honor the Lord. And if we die, it's to honor the Lord. So whether we live or die, we belong to the Lord."
– Romans 14:8

# Affirmation

My life is being lived for You. Your agenda trumps all others in my life. Everything I do is for You. It's all about You.

*Day 19*

# MY WEAKNESS EQUALS HIS STRENGTH

There are times we will feel as if we lack strength and as if we are incapable of enduring hardship. We have given our all to a person, situation, or thing, and we feel we have nothing else to give. The stress of it all has left us feeling empty and depleted to the point we have no desire to carry on. We literally want to throw in the towel and tell God and everyone else we quit. We then begin to wonder about the point of it all.

Our weaknesses are designed to make us realize that we need God. They continue to point us back to Him - the ultimate source of strength. They humble us and give us more confidence in Him because we know it is not within our own power. They make us realize we are totally relying on Him. Our weaknesses make us look at a situation and say, *now unto Him who is able.*

*God is waiting for us to stop, take a deep breath and recognize He is there with an unlimited supply of strength - strength to conquer the hard task, strength to push past the pain, and strength to face the difficult situation.* His strength is made perfect in moments like these. It allows Him the opportunity to showcase His power.

# Scriptures

"O LORD, do not stay far away! You are my
strength; come quickly to my aid!"
– Psalm 22:19

"The LORD is my strength and shield. I trust him with all
my heart. He helps me, and my heart is filled with joy. I
burst out in songs of thanksgiving. The LORD gives his people
strength. He is a safe fortress for his anointed king."
– Psalm 28:7-9

"He gives power to the weak and strength to the powerless. Even
youths will become weak and tired, and young men will fall
in exhaustion. But those who trust in the LORD will find new
strength. They will soar high on wings like eagles. They will
run and not grow weary. They will walk and not faint."
– Isaiah 40:29-31

"That's why I take pleasure in my weaknesses, and in the
insults, hardships, persecutions, and troubles that I suffer
for Christ. For when I am weak, then I am strong."
– 2 Corinthians 12:10

# Prayer

Heavenly Father, today I thank You for Your strength.
My heart is grateful because you are there to comfort me
when I am overwhelmed. In You, I have a resting place.
You will uphold, strengthen and restore me. Your strength
is perfect in my weakness. I thank You that I can run
to You when I am weak. You are my strong tower.

# *Day 20*
# LOSE CONTROL

F eeling the need to be in control is our place of comfort. We are most comfortable when we feel we are in control. We feel centered, secure, and empowered when we are in control. Some of us can only function if we are in control. We have to control our day, how a situation goes, what happens, and when it happens. The minute we lose the power of being in control, our entire world gets turned upside down.

There will be times when things happen that we have no control over. We can't fix it. We can't change it or make it disappear because it's out of our control. What happens when you lose control?

**When things get out of control, God is saying,** *let me handle it, let me fix it, let me help you with it. I am in control.* The question is, will we allow Him to take control? God knows that we need to release everything that concerns us because we don't have the power to fix it. He is just waiting for us to recognize His ability to fix it and sincerely hand it over to Him. He wants us to trust Him with it. He is waiting for us to lose control. *When we lose control, He gains control.*

# Scriptures

*"Do not be afraid or discouraged, for the LORD will personally go ahead of you. He will be with you; he will neither fail you nor abandon you."*
– Deuteronomy 31:8

*"I know that you can do anything, and no one can stop you."*
– Job 42:2

*"Have you never heard? Have you never understood? The LORD is the everlasting God, the Creator of all the earth. He never grows weak or weary. No one can measure the depths of his understanding.29 He gives power to the weak and strength to the powerless."*
– Isaiah 40:28-29

# Prayer

Today I release control of everything I have tried to fix on my own. I realize I don't have the power to fix it, but You do. You are all-powerful. You are my help and sustainer. Thank You for making every crooked path straight and removing every stumbling block. Today I lose control so that You can gain control. I place my trust in You; therefore, I will not be ashamed.

# Affirmation

You are in control of my life. You will not fail me. My world is safe with You.

*Day 21*

# MOVE PAST IT

There will always be things that cause us to rehearse our pain, disappointments, misfortunes, and everything that keeps us in a dark place. The devil wants us to rehearse and replay everything that has ever caused us misery. If we allow him to have those things on repeat in our heads, we will continue to walk around in bondage and be slaves to our own hurt.

Rehearing what someone did to you, how they treated you, or how they made you feel takes you back to that place and time and prohibits you from moving forward. God's will is that you move past every hurt and disappointment because every step you take away from it navigates you closer to your purpose.

Today, choose to move past it and renew your mind with God's word that says, forgetting the former things. You have a choice. You can continue being a slave to it, which will cause stagnation, or you can move past it, which will cause you to walk in freedom and your God-given purpose.

# Scriptures

*"Forget the former things; do not dwell on the past. See, I am doing a new thing! Now it springs up; do you not perceive it? I am making a way in the wilderness and streams in the wasteland."*
– Isaiah 43:18-19

*"Get rid of all bitterness, rage and anger, brawling and slander, along with every form of malice. Be kind and compassionate to one another, forgiving each other, just as in Christ God forgave you."*
– Ephesians 4:31-32

# Affirmation

I choose to move past every hurt and disappointment. I am free from the tormenting thoughts of my past pain. I no longer rehearse my misfortune. I am thinking on whatsoever is true, honest, just, pure, lovely, and things that are a good report.

# Day 22

# HISTORY SAYS

When we look at history, we are looking at and studying things that have occurred in the past. We look at patterns, trends, and how things have changed over time. History is often studied to predict the future so that planning can occur.

You will have seasons in your life where you don't know what to do, and you don't know your ups from your downs. It's a season that God often puts you through to increase your faith and build your confidence in Him.

When you are in the middle of a difficult season, you should look back at your history with God. Meaning you should look back at all the things He has already done. Think of the times He provided. The times He comforted you when your heart was hurting. The times He directed your path. The times He healed you. *Looking back at your history with God will renew your strength. Renewed strength equals renewed confidence.*

History says He is faithful, consistent, dependable, and committed to us. He has proven himself to be unwavering.

## Scriptures

*"The faithful love of the LORD never ends! His mercies never cease. Great is his faithfulness; His mercies begin afresh each morning."*
– Lamentations 3:22-23

*"Understand, therefore, that the LORD your God is indeed God. He is the faithful God who keeps his covenant for a thousand generations and lavishes his unfailing love on those who love him and obey his commands."*
- Deuteronomy 7:9

## Affirmation

I believe in Your power to rescue me from every situation. I believe that You are for me, and You are making all grace abound toward me. I believe You will never forsake me and that I can continue to look to You as my source. You are the answer to it all.

# Day 23

# SEEING ME THE
# WAY YOU DO

## (Perfectly Flawed)

Flaws......no one wants to discuss them. Although we all have them, we don't want to dig deep, talk about or deal with them. God forbid if someone points any of our flaws out. We become uncomfortable if they are pointed out because it reminds us that they are there and we need to deal with them.

Flaws are our weaknesses or things that we least desire about ourselves. Sometimes we will sit and take inventory of our flaws and allow them to blind us from seeing our "authentic selves." *The enemy will remind us of our imperfections, limitations, deficiencies, fears, and everything we struggle with. He wants us to see ourselves as so flawed that we feel inadequate and unqualified to be used by God.* When the truth is, our flaws are what qualify us.

Our flaws humble us and remind us that we need the God of Grace. They also allow us to empathize with others who need the God of Grace. This opens the opportunity for us to draw others and extend the love and grace that God freely gave us.

So, the next time the enemy tries to replay every one of your flaws, remind him that they are what qualify you. Then choose to see yourself the way God sees you: competent, full of faith, complete, fearfully and wonderfully made, loved, and forgiven.

# Scriptures

*"You made all the delicate, inner parts of my body and knit me together in my mother's womb. Thank you for making me so wonderfully complex! Your workmanship is marvelous—how well I know it."*
– Psalm 139:13-14

*"For we are God's masterpiece. He has created us anew in Christ Jesus, so we can do the good things he planned for us long ago."*
– Ephesians 2:10

*"Now, most people would not be willing to die for an upright person, though someone might perhaps be willing to die for a person who is especially good. But God showed his great love for us by sending Christ to die for us while we were still sinners."*
– Romans 5:7-8

# Affirmation

I am fearfully and wonderfully made. My flaws qualify me. His love and grace have freed me. God has approved of me to do a good work.

*Day 24*

# THORNS

A thorn is something that constantly annoys you and causes you to be in pain. It will put you in distress and agony because it acts relentlessly. It repeatedly reminds you that it is there. It will demand your attention by taking your focus. It is constantly screaming FOCUS ON ME!

Everyone has something that acts as a thorn in their flesh. Something that brings them pain and discomfort. We wish it would disappear. We wish it never existed. We even question the purpose of it and have questions like, *Why is it there? Is it necessary? Why did God give it to me? Why can't God just give it to someone else? Why does it cause so much pain? How long will it be there?*

Paul pleaded three times for God to remove his thorn, and God denied it and replied that His grace was sufficient for him and that His power is made perfect in our weakness. **God's power is displayed best in weakness.** In our weakness, we come to know Him as God Almighty - the One All-Powerful God. We then come to know that nothing is too difficult for Him.

Embrace the thorns. God gives some thorns. He gives thorns to humble us, to remind us that we need Him, and to keep us cognitive of His ability to save us. Thorns are painful but serve an important purpose.

# Scriptures

*"Three different times, I begged the Lord to take it away. Each time he said, 'My grace is all you need. My power works best in weakness.' So now I am glad to boast about my weaknesses so that the power of Christ can work through me."*
– 2 Corinthians 12:8-9

*"Endure suffering along with me, as a good soldier of Christ Jesus."*
– 2 Timothy 2:3

# Affirmation

I will endure hardship as a good soldier. I will allow You to be God in my life. I trust Your ways and Your plan. Even in adversity, I will look to You.

*Day 25*

# REPRESENT

As representatives of Christ, we should constantly be examining ourselves. Proper examination of ourselves will alleviate the need for others to examine us. We should examine ourselves to ensure we are appropriately representing Him and living a life aligned with His word. Our lives should represent Him and lead others to Christ.

When people see us, they should see and feel God. The love of God should be demonstrated so strongly in our lives that others should feel His love flowing from our hearts. When we speak, they should hear the voice of God. Something inside them should resonate and say, *I know God sent them to me.* There will be no questions about who placed us in their life because they are fully persuaded that we belong to God and are assigned to assist them. **When we properly represent God, everyone around us benefits. Properly representing God will attract those in need of something to us. We become magnets.**

People will be drawn to us because they know coming into contact with us is like coming into contact with Him. We have become His hands, feet, and mouthpiece. We live our lives for Him, and it is evident. The goal is to strive to represent Him in all that we say and do.

# Scriptures

*"Imitate God, therefore, in everything you do because you are his dear children. Live a life filled with love, following the example of Christ. He loved us and offered himself as a sacrifice for us, a pleasing aroma to God."*
– Ephesians 5:1-2

*"But you are not like that, for you are a chosen people. You are royal priests, a holy nation, God's very own possession. As a result, you can show others the goodness of God, for he called you out of the darkness into his wonderful light."*
– 1 Peter 2:9

*"So we are Christ's ambassadors; God is making his appeal through us. We speak for Christ when we plead, 'Come back to God!'"*
– 2 Corinthians 5:20

# Affirmation

My light shines for You. My life points people to You. I am Your representative. My life is for You and Your personal use.

# Day 26

# GOD'S PERSPECTIVE

### (Having Clear Vision)

I f we look at things through the natural eye, we often lose sight of what God is doing and saying and His purpose for our lives. We must will our spirits to see things the way He sees them. *Clear vision is seeing things from God's perspective. When we look at things from His perspective, we see His plan and purpose clearly.*

Seeing things God's way means how He feels about something is how we feel about it. The way He thinks about something is the way we think about it. His perspective plays the biggest part in how we think, feel, and move. He has the greatest influence over us because being in His image is our goal.

# Scriptures

*"Who can know the Lord's thoughts?*
*Who knows enough to teach him"*
– 1 Corinthians 2:16

*"'My thoughts are nothing like your thoughts,' says the Lord.' And*
*my ways are far beyond anything you could imagine. For just*
*as the heavens are higher than the earth, so my ways are higher*
*than your ways and my thoughts higher than your thoughts."*
– Isaiah 55:8-9

# Prayer

God, let me see things from Your perspective. Give me
clear vision. Let everything that I do be centered around
You. I don't want to see things my way but Your way. I
ask that every decision that I make be acceptable in Your
sight. If something breaks Your heart, let it break mine. If
something grieves Your spirit, let it grieve mine. If You are
displeased, let me be displeased. Let Your desires be my
desires. All of my days, let me see and do things Your way.

*Day 27*

# GRACE HAS AN
# EXPIRATION DATE

We all have things that we need to do away with. Things we need to forsake and never look back at. Things God never intended for us to partake in. Things we need to ask God to help us with. These things hinder our walk with God and create a separation between God and us. Many like to call these things their "struggles," but if we call them what they really are, they are sins.

No one wants to call them that, but that's what they are called. Sin is anything that goes against the law of God. Anytime we go against what God requires, we are operating in sin. We all have sinned and missed the mark, and God has extended His grace to us. However, there are some things that we continuously and willingly partake in and expect grace to cover us. Grace does cover us, but for how long? *How long do we expect grace to cover us while we take advantage of it? Grace has an expiration date.*

As believers, God does not want us to take His grace for granted and become slaves to sin because the wages of sin are death, but the gift of God is eternal life. God is looking for us to give ourselves completely to Him, becoming a vessel of honor, a surrendered vessel to His will, putting away the things of the flesh, and becoming a slave to righteous living.

# Scriptures

*"Well then, should we keep on sinning so that God can show us more and more of his wonderful grace? Of course not! Since we have died to sin, how can we continue to live in it?"*
– Romans 6:1-2

*"Do not let sin control the way you live; do not give in to sinful desires. Do not let any part of your body become an instrument of evil to serve sin. Instead, give yourselves completely to God, for you were dead, but now you have new life. So use your whole body as an instrument to do what is right for the glory of God."*
– Romans 6:12-13

# Prayer

Heavenly Father, today I thank You for extending Your grace to me every time I missed the mark. I ask that You give me a made-up mind and heart to completely serve You and help me put away all things that go against Your word. Search me, and whatever is not like You, take it away.

# Affirmation

I will no longer willingly sin. I will no longer take Your grace for granted. I render my life as an offering to You. I am a vessel of honor.

*Day 28*

# LEAD THEM TO
# THE SOURCE

There are times when you encounter people, and you can immediately see the hurt and disappointment they are experiencing in their eyes. You see it in their continence and even hear it when they speak. It's as if you can feel the burden on their heart.

For some of us, their burdens become our burdens. We then begin to share the weight of their problems. It's ok to feel others' pain and burdens, but what are we doing with that pain and burden? Are we allowing it to be a weight on us as it is on them? Is it overtaking our life as it is overtaking their life, or are we leading them to the ultimate burden bearer?

*When people come to us with their problems, we have a Godly responsibility to lead them to the source.* God is not looking for us to say *sorry about your bad luck. I hate this is happening to you, or I wish I could help.* He is looking for us to lead them to Him. Our Godly duty is to lead them to the source we use for help, strength, peace, and all other needs - leading them through prayer, sharing what His word says about it, or simply giving them a God-inspired word of encouragement.

Many of our hardships have caused us to go to God, and we know He is the source and the answer to it all. They, too, need to know Him in that way. Once they begin to know Him in that way, they, too, will begin to draw from the well that never runs dry and know that He has an endless supply of whatever they need.

# Scriptures

*"For everything comes from him and exists by his power and is intended for his glory. All glory to him forever! Amen."*
– Romans 11:36

*"I look up to the mountains—does my help come from there? My help comes from the LORD, who made heaven and earth! He will not let you stumble; the one who watches over you will not slumber."*
– Psalm 121:1-3

# Prayer

I thank You that You are the source. All that I need, Your hands will provide. I can rely on You as an unlimited resource. As I encounter others that may be wounded, broken, or have a need, help me to point them to You. Let me be a light showing them the path to Your heart. Let me exemplify your steadfast love, bearing witness to how You provide.

# Day 29

# LET HIM FIGHT

## (Vengeance is Mine)

Sometimes it's hard to resist the urge to fight back when people have hurt or offended us. We want to take matters into our hands and inflict the same hurt and pain on them. We want them to feel what we felt and know what it feels like. Humans naturally want to repay someone the same measure they paid us, but that's not our job. It is God's job.

When we have been wronged, hurt, offended, or betrayed, we have two choices: we can allow bitterness and hate to build in our hearts and seek revenge, or we can surrender the situation over to God, resist the urge to fight back and take Him at His word when He says, "Vengeance is mine, I shall repay."

Contrary to popular belief, seeking revenge is never a good idea. His word has forbidden us to seek revenge on others. Yes, the pain may be great. Yes, the betrayal seems unbearable, and yes, your heart feels deeply wounded, but we must trust God to fight all our battles. We must take Him at His word because He knows how to fight our battles and win. It comes down to, do we trust Him enough to fight them for us?

We can trust Him to do it because He has proven Himself faithful through His word. Therefore, fret not over evildoers. Let God be your vindicator. He is the God of justice.

# Scriptures

*"I will take revenge; I will pay them back. In due time their feet will slip. Their day of disaster will arrive, and their destiny will overtake them."*
– Deuteronomy 32:35

*"And don't say, "Now I can pay them back for what they've done to me! I'll get even with them!"*
– Proverbs 24:29

*"O LORD, the God of vengeance, O God of vengeance, let your glorious justice shine forth! Arise, O Judge of the earth. Give the proud what they deserve."*
– Psalm 94:1-2

# Prayer

Heavenly Father, today I come to You asking that You give me the strength to resist the urge to fight my enemies back. Help me trust Your word that says, fret not over evil doers because they shall soon be cut off. Touch my heart and shield it from bitterness and hate. I ask that You let love and forgiveness flow from my heart and give me patience while I wait for You to vindicate me.

*Day 30*

# NO MORE SECOND GUESSING

Have you ever been invited somewhere and felt like you didn't fit in? Have you ever been in a room full of talented people and felt your gift wasn't good enough to be standing there? Have you ever sat down at a table with brilliant minds and felt uncomfortable because you felt like you did not belong there? The feeling of all that will make you want to shrink.

All of us have had feelings of inadequacy. The feeling of inadequacy will make you second-guess yourself. If we allow it, every gift God has placed inside us will be questioned.

The devil wants you to second-guess yourself so that the minute you walk into the room, you allow the spirit of comparison to minimize your gifts. **God wants to take you to the place of NO SECOND-GUESSING.** It's a place of confidence, surety, and authority, knowing that you belong here and this is your assignment.

He wants you to be assured you are equipped for the assignment and that He has qualified and placed His stamp of approval on you. His stamp of approval solidifies everything. This eliminates any second-guessing. *Once we get past second-guessing ourselves, we see the manifestation of God's power working in every gift He has placed inside us.*

# Scriptures

*"For you are a holy people, who belong to the L*ORD *your God. Of all the people on earth, the L*ORD *your God has chosen you to be his own special treasure."*
– Deuteronomy 7:6

*"But you are not like that, for you are a chosen people. You are royal priests,[g] a holy nation, God's very own possession. As a result, you can show others the goodness of God, for he called you out of the darkness into his wonderful light."*
– 1 Peter 2:9

# Affirmation

I am walking in my God-given assignment. I am walking with clarity, knowing this is where I belong. I no longer second-guess my gifts. My gifts have been approved by God.

# *Day 31*

# PUTTING HIM FIRST

What have you put before Him? What have you allowed to take His place? What are you placing your energy into more than Him? What has robbed all of your time and thoughts? We allow so many things to take our focus off of God. These things serve as a distraction and weight because they bring no joy. We allow our jobs, businesses, kids, friends, situations, and emotions to take priority over what He has said and what He has set for us to do.

With our lips, we say that we love Him and tell everyone that no one comes before Him, but our actions are screaming out loud, saying the opposite. When our actions don't coincide with what comes out of our mouths, it is simply empty words that carry no weight.

We must decide that we will no longer allow people and situations to be lifted higher than God and what He has assigned us to do. He deserves our full attention and dedication above all else. Until we decide to put Him in His rightful place, which is first, we will continue to be unproductive and constantly chase after things that bring no pleasure, which result in the feeling of emptiness.

# Scriptures

*"Think about the things of heaven, not the things of earth."*
- Colossians 3:2

*"Seek the Kingdom of God above all else, and live righteously, and he will give you everything you need."*
– Matthew 6:33

# Prayer

God, help me to seek, honor, and put You first in my life. Let Your desires for me be my desires. I don't want anything taking Your place. I ask that You rest, rule, and abide over my life and take my will.

# Day 32
# TAKE IT AWAY

J esus prayed, "Father, if you are willing, please take this cup of suffering away from me. Yet, I want your will to be done, not mine" (Luke 22:42).

Jesus prayed for the cup of suffering to be taken away from Him. Like us, He didn't want to drink from a bitter cup. He wanted God to take it away if it was His will.

We have all been in a place where we had to drink from a bitter cup and wanted God to take it away immediately. We wanted immediate relief. The only difference between Jesus and us is we probably didn't ask if it be Your will. That's the question we avoid because no one wants to willingly volunteer to drink from a bitter cup. We all know drinking from a bitter can be painful.

So, what do we do when we've been summoned to drink from a bitter cup because we've been called into the fellowship of His suffering? Our first instinct is to ask God to take it away when it actually should be a time to start rejoicing because His glory is about to be revealed.

*The fellowship of His suffering produces His glory and shows forth the sovereignty of God. When we are in the fellowship of His suffering, we come to know God more intimately and our relationship deepens.* Our suffering often draws us closer to Him. During this time, we learn Him as the God who will give us victory.

# Scriptures

"Yes, and everyone who wants to live a godly life
in Christ Jesus will suffer persecution."
– 2 Timothy 3:12

"In his kindness, God called you to share in his eternal
glory by means of Christ Jesus. So after you have suffered
a little while, he will restore, support, and strengthen
you, and he will place you on a firm foundation."
– 1 Peter 5:10

"We can rejoice, too, when we run into problems and trials,
for we know that they help us develop endurance. And
endurance develops strength of character, and character
strengthens our confident hope of salvation."
– Romans 5:3-4

"Dear friends, don't be surprised at the fiery trials you are
going through, as if something strange were happening to you.
Instead, be very glad—for these trials make you partners with
Christ in his suffering, so that you will have the wonderful
joy of seeing his glory when it is revealed to all the world."
– 1 Peter 4:12-13

# Prayer

Father, today instead of coming to You asking You to remove every burden from me, I come to thank You for giving me the strength to withstand every fiery dart. I thank You for not allowing the pressure to cause me to lose sight of who You are and Your ability to rescue me from every situation. I thank You that those who suffer with You shall reign with You. I thank You that when I am in the middle of all my hardships, You are there in the midst, giving me strength. That's when You are the closest. I thank You that during those times, Your presence is hovering over me, so tangible that I can feel Your embrace. I ask that You keep my heart and mind stayed on You and strengthen me to wait on You until You see me through.

# Day 33

# WHAT ARE YOU EATING?

What we feed our bodies will determine our overall health. If we feed our bodies a healthy diet that consists of all the right things, they will grow strong, healthy, and have longevity. If we feed our bodies things that are full of sugar, high in cholesterol and sodium, our bodies will not grow strong and healthy. Instead, they will begin to become symptomatic with ailments.

Same thing with our spirit. If we feed it the right things, it will grow and become strong. It will be healthy and whole. If we don't feed our spirits the right things, we won't see growth and strength because they will be weak, stagnant, and malnourished.

If we want our spirits to be strong and healthy, we must feed them the word of God. Faith cometh by hearing and hearing the word of God. What are you eating? People can immediately tell what type of diet you have by what you do, say, and believe. Feed your spirit the word of God daily. Spend time reading, studying, and meditating on His word. It will edify you, build you up, and cause you to know Him in a more excellent way.

# Scriptures

*"I will study your commandments and reflect on your ways.
I will delight in your decrees and not forget your word."*
– Psalm 119:15-16

*"Study this Book of Instruction continually. Meditate on it
day and night so you will be sure to obey everything written in
it. Only then will you prosper and succeed in all you do."*
– Joshua 1:8

# Affirmation

I will feed my spirit Your word. I will meditate on Your
word daily. Your word will be my daily portion. I will
allow Your word to be the final authority over my life.

# *Day 34*

# IT'S NOT MY PROBLEM -
# I GAVE IT TO GOD

There is something so liberating about giving our problems over to God. *When someone truly realizes it's not their problem and gives it to God, freedom, peace, and newfound joy overshadow them.*

We get troubled by our troubles, but our troubles never trouble God. Many have taken on problems as their personal affliction because they have not taken God at His word. His word clearly tells us to cast all our cares upon Him. *If we neglect to cast all our cares upon Him, we take on the problem and all the side effects accompanying it.* We then allow anxiety, worry, vexation, and the feeling of uncertainty to overtake us.

Those who have discovered it's not their problem have realized that God desires to fix it for them and that He takes pleasure in fixing it; therefore, they have given it to Him knowing they can trust Him with it. They know He is there saying, *allow me to fix this for you. It's My problem, not yours.*

# Scriptures

*"Give all your worries and cares to God, for he cares about you."*
– 1 Peter 5:7

*"Be still, and know that I am God! I will be honored by every nation. I will be honored throughout the world."*
– Psalm 46:10

*"Give your burdens to the LORD, and he will take care of you. He will not permit the godly to slip and fall."*
– Psalm 55:22

# Prayer

Heavenly Father, my trust is in You. My hope is in You. I thank You for being my shield, protector, and safe place. I thank You for Your love and support during difficult times. You are my burden bearer, and I never walk through things alone. Whatever concerns me, concerns You. I appreciate You working out every problem for me and for taking every one of my problems as Your own.

# *Day 35*

# SHOW UP FOR GOD

We show up for our jobs, family members, friends, and things we want to do. We make commitments to things that we shouldn't. We say yes to things when we should be saying no. We make haste to be devoted to things that don't matter.

If we honestly pause and think about it, we show up for everyone and everything but God. Have you ever stopped to think that the Father has need of you? He needs us to get the word out about His unfailing love, to propel others to come, to be a light in the darkness, and speak words of edification into the lives of those that have lost hope. When will we show up for God to do that?

How will people know Him if we don't show them? People see, feel, and experience God through His servants. Many will not know Him or His ways until we demonstrate them. We should be a reflection of Him, drawing others and exemplifying His love. Instead, we are busy being committed to everything but our commitment to Him.

If we kept our commitment to Him, our lives would be poured out to Him and for His use. *What does a poured-out life look like? It's a life that gives and sacrifices all for the assignment God has assigned them to. It's a life that offers their life as an offering.* Simply put, it's a life that shows up for God.

# Scriptures

"Work willingly at whatever you do, as though you were
working for the Lord rather than for people. Remember
that the Lord will give you an inheritance as your reward,
and that the Master you are serving is Christ."
– Colossians 3:23-24

"So, my dear brothers and sisters, be strong and immovable.
Always work enthusiastically for the Lord, for you know
that nothing you do for the Lord is ever useless."
– 1 Corinthians 15:58

"For we are both God's workers. And you are
God's field. You are God's building."
– 1 Corinthians 3:9

# Prayer

Heavenly Father, I ask that You forgive me for showing
up for everything and everybody but not showing up to
do the things I committed myself to do for You. Today
I make You a priority and dedicate myself to You. My
heart is yielded, willing, and ready to serve You.

*Day 36*

# GET IN THE PRESS

L ife has a way of making you feel overwhelmed, stressed, fearful, and alone, leaving you with questions about your decisions, purpose, future, and very existence. The enemy uses unanswered questions to plant seeds of uncertainty and fear in you. This tactic blocks and stops you from reaching your purpose.

*If the enemy can overwhelm you, you can't think clearly. If he can paralyze you with fear, you won't make any moves. If he can make you feel alone or like you are the only one, you will begin to walk in self-pity.*

In times like these, you have to press. Press beyond being overwhelmed and the fear of it all. Even when tears fill your eyes, pressing is still required. Let the tears flow as a sign of your liquid prayers, but know He is near. He is as close as the mention of His name. He is there to strengthen and carry you through every obstacle you face. He counts it an honor to come to your aid. He shows up to do what you can't do.

God is challenging you. Psalm 11:5 speaks of the Lord testing the righteous. This is done to see which way they will go. Will you press through it all, be like Job, and declare that you will come out as pure gold?

Accept the challenge and press through everything that is stopping and hindering you from trusting God. It has been proven that we can trust Him with our lives, purpose, problems, and everything that concerns us.

# Scriptures

"No, dear brothers and sisters, I have not achieved it, but I focus on this one thing: Forgetting the past and looking forward to what lies ahead, I press on to reach the end of the race and receive the heavenly prize for which God, through Christ Jesus, is calling us."
– Philippians 3:13-14

"So let's not get tired of doing what is good. At just the right time, we will reap a harvest of blessing if we don't give up."
– Galatians 6:9

# Prayer

Lord, I am asking that when I face obstacles or disappointments, You don't allow them to crush me or make me quit, but make my feet like hinds feet, able to stand, so that I can continue to press. I thank You that I won't bend under pressure, but I will press and focus on Your word, which declares me victorious.

# Affirmation

You have made my feet like hinds feet. I can face anything as long as I have You. You are for me. Not against me. You came to do me good. I have everything I need to face adversities because I have You.

# *Day 37*

# ENOUGH ALREADY

Some things will never change until it has exhausted us to the point where there is no other option but to change. No other option but to forsake and put away what is hindering us from being our best selves and reaching our God-given potential.

Sometimes God will take away some things we struggle with, while other things we struggle with, we must will our spirit to put them away. We must consciously decide that it will no longer serve as a stumbling block and have power over us. Anything that controls us has power over us; therefore, we must take the power of it away.

Things will remain the same until we say, ENOUGH ALREADY. Enough of allowing distractions, fear, heartbreak, shame, feelings of inadequacy, excuses, and disobedience to hinder us. If we truly desire to honor God with our lives and feel fulfilled, we must abandon everything that goes against His will.

# Scriptures

*"Do not let sin control the way you live;[a] do not give in to sinful desires. Do not let any part of your body become an instrument of evil to serve sin. Instead, give yourselves completely to God, for you were dead, but now you have new life. So use your whole body as an instrument to do what is right for the glory of God."*
– Romans 6:12-13

*"Then Jesus said to his disciples, 'If any of you wants to be my follower, you must give up your own way, take up your cross, and follow me. If you try to hang on to your life, you will lose it. But if you give up your life for my sake, you will save it.'"*
– Matthew 16:24-25

# Prayer

Father, today I forsake everything that is hindering me. My thoughts and plans no longer matter. It's all about You and what You want to do. I surrender my will. I surrender my way. I thank You for opening the eyes of my understanding and allowing me to realize that I must abandon all hindrances. Here I am, yielded and ready.

# Day 38
# HE WON'T FAIL

God is not slack concerning His promises. He is faithful, true, and committed to us. Unlike man, He doesn't walk around handing out empty hopes and promises. His faithfulness to us is consistent and reliable.

How often have we put our hopes and trust in things that have failed us? The repeated failure of those things only disappointed us and made us realize that none compare to His faithfulness. We then know Him to be the only reliable source.

God wants us to trust Him and know He will never fail us. He is saying, "I am God almighty. I am incapable of failing. I am more than able to keep My word. You have an absolute promise in Me."

# Scriptures

"Do not be afraid or discouraged, for the LORD will personally go ahead of you. He will be with you; he will neither fail you nor abandon you."
– Deuteronomy 31:8

"The LORD makes firm the steps of the one who delights in him; though he may stumble, he will not fall, for the LORD upholds him with his hand."
– Psalm 37:23-24

"When you go through deep waters, I will be with you. When you go through rivers of difficulty, you will not drown. When you walk through the fire of oppression, you will not be burned up; the flames will not consume you."
– Isaiah 43:2

# Prayer

Heavenly Father, Your word says You will never leave or forsake me. I thank You for being a reliable source. You are so dependable. You have always kept Your word. Your word never returns void. I place my trust in You and You only because there is no failure in You. I ask that You always let me look to You whenever I am going through. I thank You for always showing Yourself strong in my life.

# Affirmation

I place all of my hope in You. You are a firm foundation. I have tested and tried You. I am confident that You have me covered.

# Day 39

# HIS STANDARDS

S ociety tries to dictate what we should look like, how we should feel, what we should think, our choices, and what we should do. If we allow it, society will shape us into the person they want us to be. We will then begin to think, feel, and be what they feel is acceptable - judging ourselves to their standard.

Who said society's standards are correct? We should only judge ourselves according to God's standards. His standard is His word. Judging everything against what He considers right, acceptable, and holy is a walk of obedience. *When we walk in obedience, we are on one accord with Him.*

We must put away the things that society deems acceptable and let the goal be to meet His standards. *A heart that seeks to meet His standards is a heart yielded for His personal use.*

## Scripture

*"For the sinful nature is always hostile to God. It never did obey God's laws, and it never will. That's why those who are still under the control of their sinful nature can never please God. But you are not controlled by your sinful nature. You are controlled by the Spirit if you have the Spirit of God living in you. (And remember that those who do not have the Spirit of Christ living in them do not belong to him at all)."*
– Romans 8:7-9

## Prayer

Today I come to You, bringing You my ways. I exchange my ways for Your ways. I want to meet Your standards. Lord, let me judge everything I do against Your standards. I abandon all of the standards that society had told me were right. Your way is the perfect way.

*Day 40*

# HOW WILL YOU RESPOND?

The way we respond to hardship matters. Life is going to happen. It's inevitable. Days of feeling overwhelmed, inadequate, unproductive, ineffective, and incomplete will try to make you abandon your assignment and quit. *Hardships are designed to make you throw in the towel. But if you persevere and do not make quitting an option, once again, the devil will be defeated.*

One of the things we often experience during our hardships is hopelessness. Hopelessness brings on the spirit of defeat. We feel defeated and as if we have lost the battle and have no need to persevere any longer. Giving in to hopelessness hinders us from walking in victory.

We need to realize that God is watching. He is watching to see how we will respond. When hardship hits, will we allow it to overtake us, break us, and tell God we quit, or will we gird up our faith, take Him at His word and say, "If God be for me, who can be against me?" How we respond will determine our outcome. Our response matters.

# Scriptures

*"So do not fear, for I am with you; do not be dismayed,
for I am your God. I will strengthen you and help you;
I will uphold you with my righteous right hand."*
– Isaiah 41:10

*"What, then, shall we say in response to these things?
If God is for us, who can be against us?"*
– Romans 8:31

# Prayer

I thank You for keeping me. I thank You for keeping my
mind and my heart stayed on You. When troubles come and
hard days arise, help me to respond with Your word. Let my
confession be *He is with me; I will not fear.* I thank You that
I won't faint under the pressure because You have let me
know You are near. Thank You for working things out for my
good and causing me to see Your hand move once again.

# *Day 41*

# DROP THE WEIGHT

*I*t is not God's plan for us to be bogged down, overwhelmed, and stressed with the cares of life.

Stress, being overwhelmed, overthinking, and worrying all act as weights. Weights are burdens that restrict movement. A weight serves as a hindrance to delay and prevents you from doing the things of God.

Anyone who has ever been fully persuaded and serious about doing what God has required them to do will tell you they had to drop every weight. Meaning, everything that was a burden and holding them down, they had to let it go. They realized they could not accomplish anything carrying the weight. You can't freely serve God weighted down.

There is so much that God has required us to do, but we can't because we are weighted down with things He has told us to lay aside. Once we drop every weight prohibiting us, we will begin to flourish in our God-given purpose and see the manifestation of His will for our lives.

Pause and calmly think. What things are weighing you down and causing you not to reach your purpose? Has God given you the power to change any of those things? Many of us need to evaluate, access, and re-adjust some things because God is waiting on us to release every weight.

## Scripture

*"Therefore, since we are surrounded by such a huge crowd of witnesses to the life of faith, let us strip off every weight that slows us down, especially the sin that so easily trips us up. And let us run with endurance the race God has set before us."*
— Hebrews 12:1

## Prayer

Heavenly Father, today I come to You releasing the weight of everything that has been placed in my life to serve as a hindrance. I thank You that everything that has weighted me down will no longer serve as a weight. I thank You that I will serve you with a free spirit because You have made my way easy and all my burdens light. I thank You that I will run this race **weightless** because I have casted everything that concerns me on You.

*Day 42*

# MIND SHIFT

## (Dancing In The Rain)

Have you ever had one of those days where nothing is going right? I mean, nothing is going your way. It is like from the time you wake up, there is a problem for you to face, and then after that....... there is another problem! You seem unable to catch a break because it is one thing after another. You then begin to think to yourself, *can this day get worse?* Just when you think it couldn't get worse..... It gets worse!

This is the time to shift your focus. **Shifting your focus will shift your perspective.** Stop focusing on what isn't working for you and start focusing on what is working for you. Now begin to count every blessing you can think of, and with a heart of gratitude, tell God *thank You.* Our sincere gratitude for what He has already done will cause Him to do MORE.

Things will not always go our way. The sun will not always be shining, but if we learn to do a mind shift, it will give our spirits the strength needed to persevere. Perseverance is part of enduring hardness as a good soldier. If this is mastered, you have learned how to dance in the rain.

# Scriptures

"We do this by keeping our eyes on Jesus, the champion who initiates and perfects our faith. Because of the joy awaiting him, he endured the cross, disregarding its shame. Now he is seated in the place of honor beside God's throne. Think of all the hostility he endured from sinful people; then you won't become weary and give up."
– Hebrews 12:2-3

"We can rejoice, too, when we run into problems and trials, for we know that they help us develop endurance. And endurance develops strength of character, and character strengthens our confident hope of salvation."
– Romans 5:3-4

# Prayer

Heavenly Father, thank You for still being good, even on a bad day. Father, I ask that when things don't go as planned, and it seems it won't get better, let me shift my focus. Let me focus on Your goodness, Your kindness, and Your love. I thank You that as I focus on those things, You will begin to pour strength, peace, and relentlessness into me.

# *Day 43*
# NO MORE WASTED TIME

Procrastination is the enemy of progress. How often has God given us an idea or a vision to carry out, and we take it in and do nothing with it? We talk about it but never birth it; therefore, it is only a thought. It will never become anything until we GET TO IT.

What is hindering you from GETTING TO IT? Is it laziness, fear, procrastination, or distractions? Figure out what it is and ask God to help you with it so you can carry out the things God has placed in your heart to do. Once you've figured out the things hindering you and asked God for help, GET BUSY! Some things require prayer, but others simply require discipline. It is now time to operate in discipline and get it done.

Enough time has been wasted. Do whatever your hands can find to do, working towards the vision. The urgency to move quickly with the planning and execution of the vision should be a priority. ***Slothfulness is a sin that will cause you to make excuses for not being productive and make you miss out on many God-given opportunities.*** Until the vision is completed, you have work to do. No more wasted time.

# Scriptures

"But you, lazybones, how long will you sleep? When will you wake up? A little extra sleep, a little more slumber, a little folding of the hands to rest—then poverty will pounce on you like a bandit; scarcity will attack you like an armed robber."
– Proverbs 6:9-11

"Whatever you do, do well. For when you go to the grave, there will be no work or planning or knowledge or wisdom."
– Ecclesiastes 9:10

# Prayer

Lord, I thank You for this day and for letting me know I have work to do. I ask that You put an urgency within me to get it done. I thank You that I will not be slothful in doing the things You have given me to do, but I will make haste to complete every assignment You have assigned to me. I ask that You let me do my assignments excellently and gladly as a service unto You. I thank You that after completing every assignment, I will feel the fulfillment and joy of doing Your will.

## *Day 44*

# ONE LIFE, MANY PURPOSES

Have you ever stopped to think, why am I here? What is God's plan for my life? What is the purpose of my very existence? These are questions that everyone has asked at some point. These questions are often asked when we are trying to figure out God's plan for our lives or when we are in the valley of making decisions.

We must understand that there isn't just one plan or purpose but many plans and purposes that our lives will serve. Each purpose/plan yields to the appointed season of God's timing.

To know His plan and purpose, we must stay connected to Him. Our connection to Him is vital. Our connection will give us insight into each plan He has and the appropriate timing.

What you are doing for God now is part of the plan and purpose He has for you. Five years from now, you will be in another season and most likely doing something totally different than He has assigned you to do. Guess what? That's still part of the plan and purpose He has for your life.

We have one life, but our life will serve many purposes. Trust the place He has you in now and know that when the season changes and you are on to the next thing God has for you to do, you are still in His will because your life is meant to serve many purposes.

# Scriptures

"Commit everything you do to the LORD.
Trust him, and he will help you."
– Psalm 37:5

"For I know the plans I have for you,' says the LORD. 'They are plans
for good and not for disaster, to give you a future and a hope.'"
– Jeremiah 29:11

"The LORD will work out his plans for my life—for your faithful love,
O LORD, endures forever. Don't abandon me, for you made me."
– Psalm 138:8

# Affirmation

I am where I am supposed to be. I am doing what I am supposed
to be doing. My life has many purposes. I am following God's
plan for my life. In every season of my life, I trust Him.

*Day 45*

# IN AWE

When God leaves us in "awe," we are standing in amazement, wonder, and astonishment. We are left marveling at the works of His hands, which fill our hearts with so much gratitude and admiration for Him.

If we, Selah - pause and calmly think about God and His awesomeness, we would get lost in our thoughts, and our hearts would become overwhelmed with love for Him. If we took a moment to think and list all of the things that He does daily that leave us in awe, the list would be endless. There would be no end because He is a wonder.

His daily faithfulness leaves us in awe at how committed He is to us. His ability to forgive and cast it into the sea of forgetfulness amazes us. His endless love, attentiveness to our needs, and handiwork all leave us marveling at His power.

In your quiet time, sit and focus on God. Focus on all the things He has done that have left you amazed. His ability to rescue you from any situation, His mercy, His ability to heal you from sickness and disease, and much more. As you focus on His power and all the things that leave you astounded, observe how your heart becomes full of joy and how you feel empowered with faith and amazed by His love.

# Scriptures

*"Who is like you among the gods, O LORD — glorious in
holiness, awesome in splendor, performing great wonders?"*
– Exodus 15:11

*"Those who live at the ends of the earth stand in awe of your wonders.
From where the sun rises to where it sets, you inspire shouts of joy."*
– Psalm 65:8

*"The LORD replied, 'Listen, I am making a covenant with you
in the presence of all your people. I will perform miracles that
have never been performed anywhere in all the earth or in any
nation. And all the people around you will see the power of
the LORD —the awesome power I will display for you.'"*
– Exodus 34:10

# Affirmation

I will forever think of You and the things You do
to amaze me. Flowing from my heart will always be
gratitude. I will never lose my sense of wonder.